Success Tweets

For Sales Professionals

140 Bits of Common Sense
Sales Career Advice
All in 140 Characters or Less

BUD BILANICH
The Common Sense Guy

FRONT ROW PRESS

Front Row Press
191 University Boulevard, #414 • Denver, CO 80206 • 303.393.0446

As always, this book is for Cathy

xoxoxoxoxoxoxoxoxoxoxoxoxoxoxoxoxoxoxoxoxoxoxoxo
xoxoxoxoxoxoxoxoxoxoxoxoxoxoxoxoxoxoxoxoxoxoxoxo
xoxoxoxoxoxoxoxoxoxoxoxoxoxoxoxoxoxoxoxoxoxoxoxo
xoxoxoxoxoxoxoxoxoxoxoxoxoxoxoxoxoxoxoxoxoxoxoxo
xoxoxoxoxoxoxoxoxoxoxoxoxoxoxoxoxoxoxoxoxoxoxoxo
xoxoxoxoxoxoxoxoxoxoxoxoxoxoxoxoxoxoxoxoxoxoxoxo
xoxoxoxoxoxoxoxoxoxoxoxoxoxoxoxoxoxoxoxoxoxoxoxo

That's 140 hugs and kisses…

Introduction

This is a success book in 140 tweets. It's a real book that will help you create the sales professional success you deserve.

It gives you 140 pieces of common sense sales professional success advice, all in 140 characters or less.

It will tell you how to succeed as a sales professional, 1 tweet at a time. You'll get the essentials with no fluff.

Becoming a highly successful sales professional should be fun and exciting. This book will show you how to do it.

Your time is valuable. You don't want to waste it. That's why you get 140 pieces of advice twitter style, in 140 characters or less.

Building a successful sales professional career is simple common sense. It's not hard, but you need to do it right.

Focus on the 8 Keys to becoming a successful sales professional.

Clarify the purpose and direction for your life and career.

- Create clarity by figuring out what success means to you personally.
- Create clarity by creating a vivid mental image of yourself as a success.
- Create clarity by determining your personal values.

Commit to your sales professional success.

- Take personal responsibility.
- Take personal responsibility by setting and achieving high goals.

- Take personal responsibility by choosing to react positively to the people and events in your life; especially the negative ones.

Build unshakable self confidence.

- Build your confidence by choosing to be optimistic.
- Build your confidence by facing your fears and acting.
- Build your confidence by surrounding yourself with positive people.
- Build your confidence by finding a mentor to help you create your success.

Get competent.

- Get competent by becoming a lifelong learner.
- Get competent by getting fit.

- Get competent by managing your time, life and stress well.
- Get competent by learning what it takes to become a successful sales professional.

Create positive personal impact.

- Create positive personal impact by creating and nurturing your unique personal brand.
- Create positive personal impact by being impeccable in your presentation of self; in person and on line.
- Create positive personal impact by knowing and following the basic rules of business etiquette.

Become a dynamic communicator.

- Become a dynamic communicator by demonstrating strong conversation skills.

- Become a dynamic communicator by writing clearly and succinctly.
- Become a dynamic communicator by mastering public speaking skills.

Build strong relationships.

- Build relationships through self awareness. Use this knowledge to better understand others.
- Build relationships by paying it forward; give with no expectation of return.
- Build relationships by using conflict to strengthen, not weaken, relationships with the important people in your life.

Take care of yourself.

- Do what you need to feel good about yourself, your life and your career.

The tweets that follow will show you how to put these 8 Keys to work — and become the successful sales pro you deserve to be.

Will tweet books replace traditional books? Probably not. But this book will get you started as a successful sales pro.

Enjoy this book. But remember, I want to talk *with* you, not *to* you. Please tweet what you think about my ideas. @BudBilanich.

Each of the points I've made above is less than 140 characters.

See? You can communicate a lot of useful information in 140 characters or less. Enjoy the following 140 tweets.

Clarity

CLARITY

1

Define exactly what becoming a successful sales pro means to you. It's easier to hit a clear, unambiguous target.

CLARITY

2

The more clear you are about what sales success means to you personally, the easier it will be to create the life you want.

CLARITY

3

Think of your purpose as your personal mission; why you are on this earth. Your direction is your vision for the next 3 to 5 years.

CLARITY

4

The mightier your purpose, the more likely you are to succeed. It will give you a strong foundation when the winds of change shift.

CLARITY

5

Your vision should be a BHAG; a Big Hairy Audacious Goal. Make it something that is really worth working for and accomplishing.

CLARITY

6

Make sure you really want to be a sales pro. Work you love will make it easier to create the success you deserve.

CLARITY

7

Don't focus just on making money. If you
do, you'll be asking too little of yourself.
Focus on being useful in this world.

CLARITY

8

Happiness doesn't come from getting more things. It comes from finding a worthy purpose and pursuing it.

CLARITY

9

Emerson says, "Good luck is another name for tenacity of purpose." Pursue your purpose as a sales pro tenaciously.

CLARITY

10

Create a vivid mental image of your success. This vivid image will keep you motivated and moving forward when things get tough.

CLARITY

11

Think of your vivid mental image as a blueprint. It is a plan for success, but you still have to do the work to make it a reality.

CLARITY

12

Visualize the euphoria of your sales pro success, not the pain of failure.

CLARITY

13

Use affirmations to create your sales success. Affirmations are statements about the future stated in the present tense.

CLARITY

14

Clarify your personal values. They are your anchor and your guide to decision making in ambiguous situations.

CLARITY

15

Your values come from deep inside you. Spend the time necessary to discover them. Hold fast to them; honor them by your actions.

Commitment

COMMITMENT

16

You're in charge! Commit to taking personal responsibility for becoming the successful sales pro you deserve to be.

COMMITMENT

17

Take personal responsibility for your success. No one will do it for you. Remember: "If it's to be, it's up to me."

COMMITMENT

18

Aim high. Set and achieve high goals —
month after month and year after year
after year. Do whatever it takes to achieve
those goals.

COMMITMENT

19

Make your goals S.M.A.R.T. : **S**pecific, **M**easurable, **A**chievable, **R**elevant and **T**ime Bound.

COMMITMENT

20

Focus on your goals several times a day. Spend your valuable time only on the things that will help you achieve them.

COMMITMENT

21

List the reasons for each goal you set for yourself. These reasons will come in handy you when you get tired and frustrated.

COMMITMENT

22

Create goals in all areas of your life: career, personal, business, family, hobbies, health and fitness. Make sure they are congruent.

COMMITMENT

23

Plan how you will achieve your sales professional goals. Do whatever you have to do, not feel like doing, to achieve them.

COMMITMENT

24

Stuff will happen as you create your sales professional success. Choose to respond positively to the negative stuff.

COMMITMENT

25

Failures are the tuition you pay for success. When you have a setback, choose to react positively and learn something.

COMMITMENT

26

Persistent people keep going; especially in the face of difficulties. Keep at it; you will reach your sales professional goals.

COMMITMENT

27

Don't be afraid to fail. You fail only if you don't learn something from the experience. Treat every failure as an opportunity to grow.

COMMITMENT

28

It's not what happens to you, but how you react to it. Don't dwell on the negative, use it as a springboard to action and creativity.

COMMITMENT

29

Don't let a slow day get you down. If you come back empty handed in your quest for success, get up the next day and keep working.

COMMITMENT

30

Vision without action is a daydream. No matter how big your plans and dreams, they'll never become a reality until you act on them.

Confidence

CONFIDENCE

31

Focus on what you are becoming — a successful sales professional. This makes it easier to believe in yourself.

CONFIDENCE

32

Choose optimism. It builds your confidence. Believe that today will be better than yesterday and that tomorrow will be better yet.

CONFIDENCE

33

Optimism is contagious. Become a positive, optimistic person. Surround yourself with positive people. They will build your confidence.

CONFIDENCE

34

Everyone is afraid sometime. Self confident people face their fears and act. Look your fears in the eye and do something.

CONFIDENCE

35

Defeat fear. Here are 4 steps to deal with fears that can sabotage your success. Identify it. Admit it. Accept it. Do something about it.

CONFIDENCE

36

Procrastination is the physical manifestation of fear and is a confidence killer. Act — especially when you're afraid.

CONFIDENCE

37

Surround yourself with positive people. Hold them close. They will give you energy and help you create the success you want and deserve.

CONFIDENCE

38

Jettison the negative people in your life. They are energy black holes. They will suck you dry; but only if you let them.

CONFIDENCE

39

Find a mentor; a person who will help you find the lessons in your problems and failures and how to use them to move forward.

CONFIDENCE

40

Identify the self confident people you know. Pay attention to how they act and carry themselves. Watch what they do. Act like them.

CONFIDENCE

41

Fake it till you make it. Act as if you expect to be accepted, and you will be. This will boost your self confidence!

CONFIDENCE

42

Self confidence comes from within. Outside reinforcement and strokes can help, but you have to build your own confidence.

CONFIDENCE

43

Be as enthusiastic about the success of others as you are about your own. Help all the people around you recognize that they are special.

CONFIDENCE

44

Give so much time to building your self confidence and improving yourself that you have no time to criticize others.

CONFIDENCE

45

Take stock of yourself. What are your strengths? What are your weaknesses? Confident people emphasize their strengths.

Competence

COMPETENCE

46

Become a lifelong learner. The half-life of knowledge is rapidly diminishing. Staying in the same place is the same as going backwards.

COMPETENCE

47

Learn as fast, or faster, than the world changes. In a world that never stops changing, you can never stop learning and growing.

COMPETENCE

48

Stay focused. Don't get distracted. Treat time as the precious commodity that it is. Manage your time and life well.

COMPETENCE

49

Break large projects into smaller chunks.
They are not so overwhelming that way.
Set mini milestones for yourself.

COMPETENCE

50

Get organized. Organize your time, life and workspace. Sweat the small stuff. Success is in execution. Execution is in the details.

COMPETENCE

51

The better you feel, the better you'll perform. Live a healthy lifestyle. Eat well. Exercise regularly. Get regular checkups.

COMPETENCE

52

Determine your peak energy times.
Schedule "high brain" tasks then and "low
brain" tasks at times when your energy is
lowest.

COMPETENCE

53

Don't take yourself too seriously. Lighten up. It will help you master yourself and become an outstanding sales pro.

COMPETENCE

54

Get into a high performance mindset. Don't question yourself. Trust your skills and abilities. Do what you know how to do.

COMPETENCE

55

Good truly is the enemy of great. Don't settle for good performance. Today, good is mediocre. Become a great performer.

COMPETENCE

56

Always get to know your customer and his or her needs before you try to sell anything.

COMPETENCE

57

Know exactly what you are going to say
when you begin any sales call. A strong,
confident opening will lead to more sales.

COMPETENCE

58

Build relationships constantly and continuously. Keep in touch via phone, email, text messages and the occasional handwritten note.

COMPETENCE

59

Develop TOMA with your customers —
Top Of the Mind Awareness. Make sure
they think of you first.

COMPETENCE

60

Make sure you know the value of your goods or services from your customers' perspective. Sell specific benefits to specific customers.

COMPETENCE

61

Enter each call with a specific outcome in mind. It may be relationship building. It may be information sharing. It may be closing.

COMPETENCE

62

Adjust your selling style to the customer. Don't expect him or her to adjust to you and your style.

COMPETENCE

63

People buy because you can solve a problem for them. Figure out their problems. Then design your presentation.

COMPETENCE

64

Reflect on every call. What went right?
What went wrong? What will you do
better next time?

COMPETENCE

65

Build relationships with other sales pros in your company. They can help you through the tough times that always come with selling.

COMPETENCE

66

Build relationships outside of your company. Your network will help you with the connections you need to become a top sales pro.

COMPETENCE

67

Become a top notch storyteller. Use stories to illustrate both the features and benefits of your products and services.

COMPETENCE

68

Selling skills need constant practice and rejuvenation. Role play with your sales manager and other sales pros to sharpen your skills.

COMPETENCE

69

Focus on your strengths. They are the source of your personal power as a sales pro. Always come from a position of strength.

COMPETENCE

70

Do what works. Evaluate your calls. Pay attention to what works and what doesn't. Keep doing what works. Stop doing what doesn't.

COMPETENCE

71

Change with the times. What worked yesterday may not work today or tomorrow. Adapt and grow. Keep your skills up to date.

COMPETENCE

72

Know your competitors' products as well or better than you know your own.

COMPETENCE

73

Ask your best customers to help with referrals. Ask for something specific — an introduction, a phone call, a lunch or breakfast.

COMPETENCE

74

Get information before you give it.
Always let the customer speak first. He or she will give you important cues that will help you close the sale.

COMPETENCE

75

Be passionate and enthusiastic. No one will buy from you if you aren't excited about what you're selling.

COMPETENCE

76

Face to face sales time is precious. Make sure you take full advantage of the gift of time your customer gives you.

COMPETENCE

77

Script out what you'll say as you begin a call. The first minute is very important. Make sure you take charge positively.

COMPETENCE

78

Get your customers to think of you as their "go to" expert — the person who understands their issues and how to address them.

COMPETENCE

79

Follow up. You won't make many sales on the first call. Persistence and follow up are the key to selling.

COMPETENCE

80

Avoid complacency. Every call is a new and unique opportunity to demonstrate your ability to satisfy your customers' needs.

COMPETENCE

81

Always go beyond what is expected. Give your customers extraordinary value and service.

COMPETENCE

82

Use technology to enhance, not drive your presentation. Don't lose your message in the bells and whistles.

COMPETENCE

83

A strong product brand is no substitute for sloppy sales habits. Always present yourself as the polished sales pro you are.

COMPETENCE

84

Always send a handwritten thank you note as soon as you make a sale. You'll stand out from your competition.

COMPETENCE

85

Stay positive. Selling is tough. Treat your setbacks as the tuition you pay for sales success.

Positive Personal Impact

POSITIVE PERSONAL IMPACT

86

Create and nurture your unique personal brand. Stand, and be known for, something. Make sure that everything you do is on brand.

POSITIVE PERSONAL IMPACT

87

Your personal brand should be unique to you, but built on integrity. Integrity is doing the right thing even when no one's looking.

POSITIVE PERSONAL IMPACT

88

Build your personal brand. Do whatever it takes to make sure that people will think of and remember you in the way you want them to.

POSITIVE PERSONAL IMPACT

89

Nurture your network. What your friends, colleagues, clients, and customers say about you is how others will think of your brand.

POSITIVE PERSONAL IMPACT

90

Demonstrate respect for yourself and others in your dress. People will notice and respond positively to you.

POSITIVE PERSONAL IMPACT

91

Be well groomed and appropriate for every situation. Always dress one level up from what is expected. You'll stand out from the crowd.

POSITIVE PERSONAL IMPACT

92

"Business" is the first and most important word in "business casual". Dress like you're going to work, not a sporting event or club.

POSITIVE PERSONAL IMPACT

93

21st Century technology has created new etiquette rules. Learn and use them to appear polished when you're on line.

POSITIVE PERSONAL IMPACT

94

Be gracious. Know and follow the basic rules of etiquette. Everybody likes to be around polite and mannerly people.

POSITIVE PERSONAL IMPACT

95

When someone compliments you, just say "thank you." When someone criticizes you, say "thank you, I'll work on that".

POSITIVE PERSONAL IMPACT

96

Learn and use simple table manners.
Good manners make you look polished
and poised and help you concentrate on
the conversation.

POSITIVE PERSONAL IMPACT

97

Always act like a lady or gentleman. It's not old fashioned; it's smart business and leads to a successful life and career.

POSITIVE PERSONAL IMPACT

98

Keep your breath fresh. Brush after meals and coffee. Use the strips. Don't chew gum. Ever. It makes you look like a cow.

POSITIVE PERSONAL IMPACT

99

Say "thank you" often. You'll succeed in your life and career, build a strong personal brand and leave a legacy of being a nice person.

POSITIVE PERSONAL IMPACT

100

Be courteous. It costs you nothing, and it can mean everything to someone else. It also helps in getting what you want.

Dynamic Communication

DYNAMIC COMMUNICATION

101

All dynamic communicators have mastered three basic communication skills: conversation, writing and presenting.

DYNAMIC COMMUNICATION

102

Speak from your heart. Show that you care — about yourself and the people with whom you are speaking.

DYNAMIC COMMUNICATION

103

A brief conversation with the right person can greatly help — or hinder your success as a sales pro.

DYNAMIC COMMUNICATION

104

Conversation tips: be warm, pleasant, gracious and sensitive to the interpersonal needs and anxieties of others.

DYNAMIC COMMUNICATION

105

Demonstrate your understanding of others' points of view. Listen well and ask questions if you don't understand.

DYNAMIC COMMUNICATION

106

Become an excellent conversationalist by listening more than speaking. Pay attention to what other people say; respond appropriately.

DYNAMIC COMMUNICATION

107

Live people take precedence over phone calls. So continue in person, face to face conversations, rather than answering your cell phone.

108

Use the 2/3 - 1/3 rule. Listen two thirds of the time; speak one third of the time. Focus your complete attention on the other person.

DYNAMIC COMMUNICATION

109

Remember and use people's names. Look for common ground with the people you meet. Find out about them, their hobbies and passions.

DYNAMIC COMMUNICATION

110

Become a clear, concise writer. Make your writing easy to read and easy to understand. Use simple straightforward language.

111

Write clearly and simply: short words and sentences; first person; active voice. Be precise in your choice of words.

112

Become an excellent presenter. Script your talk. Practice until you are perfect.

DYNAMIC COMMUNICATION

113

Presentation steps: 1) Determine the message. 2) Analyze the audience. 3) Organize the information. 4) Design visuals. 5) Practice.

DYNAMIC COMMUNICATION

114

Presentations are easy to create. Write your closing first, your opening next. Then fill in the content. Practice, practice, practice.

DYNAMIC COMMUNICATION

115

Discipline yourself to prepare for presentations. Practice out loud until you are totally in sync with what you're going to say.

Relationship Building

RELATIONSHIP BUILDING

116

Get genuinely interested in others. Help bring out the best in everyone you know. Others will gravitate to you.

RELATIONSHIP BUILDING

117

Use every social interaction to build and strengthen relationships. Strong relationships are your ticket to success as a sales pro.

RELATIONSHIP BUILDING

118

Everyone has something to offer. Never dismiss anyone out of hand. Take the initiative. Actively build relationships with others.

RELATIONSHIP BUILDING

119

Get to know yourself. Use your self knowledge to better understand others and build mutually beneficial relationships with them.

RELATIONSHIP BUILDING

120

Pay it forward. Build relationships by giving with no expectation of return. Give of yourself to build strong relationships.

RELATIONSHIP BUILDING

121

When meeting someone new ask yourself, "What can I do to help this person?" By thinking this first, you'll build stronger relationships.

RELATIONSHIP BUILDING

122

There is no quid pro quo in effective relationships. Do for others without being asked or waiting for them to do for you.

RELATIONSHIP BUILDING

123

Be generous. By giving with no expectation of return, you'll be surprised by how much comes back to you in the long run.

RELATIONSHIP BUILDING

124

Be happy to see others succeed. Use the success of others to motivate yourself to greater success.

RELATIONSHIP BUILDING

125

Trust is the glue that holds relationships together. The more you demonstrate trust in others, the more they will trust you.

RELATIONSHIP BUILDING

126

Resolve conflict positively. Treat conflict as an opportunity to strengthen, not destroy, the relationships you've worked hard to build.

RELATIONSHIP BUILDING

127

Be a consensus builder. Focus on where you agree with other people. It will be easier to resolve differences and create agreement.

RELATIONSHIP BUILDING

128

Be responsible for yourself. No one can "make you angry". Choose to act in a civil, forthright, constructive manner in tense situations.

RELATIONSHIP BUILDING

129

We all make mistakes. Own up to yours. You'll become known as a straight shooter — honest with yourself and with others.

RELATIONSHIP BUILDING

130

Become widely trusted. Deliver on what you say you'll do. If you can't meet a commitment, let the other person know right away.

Take Care
Of Yourself

TAKE CARE OF YOURSELF

131

Be kind to yourself. Accept yourself. Love yourself and who you are.

TAKE CARE OF YOURSELF

132

Take care of yourself. Do what you need to do to feel good about yourself, your life and your sales professional career.

TAKE CARE OF YOURSELF

133

Choose to be you — don't wait for other people's permission to live your life and pursue your sales pro success.

TAKE CARE OF YOURSELF

134

Be hopeful and abundant. Hope defeats
fear. Abundance defeats scarcity.

TAKE CARE OF YOURSELF

135

You get what you expect. Expect the best as a sales pro and you'll get it.

TAKE CARE OF YOURSELF

136

When you focus on what's going right in your life, things will begin going right more often.

TAKE CARE OF YOURSELF

137

Blame, resentments and envy get in the way of taking care of yourself and creating the sales success you deserve.

TAKE CARE OF YOURSELF

138

Forgiveness precedes peace and harmony. Forgive others. More important, forgive yourself.

TAKE CARE OF YOURSELF

139

Every morning when you wake up, envision yourself as having a great day, filled with success and happiness.

TAKE CARE OF YOURSELF

140

Every night before you go to sleep, think about the good things that happened to you that day. Sleep in appreciation of them.

141

And, because I always over deliver, here is one more very important tweet…

Knowing is not enough. Successful sales pros will act on this advice. Take action. Become the successful sales pro I know you can be.

About Bud Bilanich

@BudBilanich, a life and career success coach helping you create the success you deserve. Let me help you succeed: www.BudBilanich.com.

Success Tweets for Sales Professionals
makes a great gift!

Quantity discounts are available
from the publisher.

Call 303.393.0446 to inquire
about quantity pricing.

www.ingramcontent.com/pod-product-compliance
Lightning Source LLC
La Vergne TN
LVHW051519080426
835509LV00017B/2119